Getting Over John Doe

A Story of Love,

Heartache, and

Surviving with Style

Getting Over
John Doe

Suzanne Yalof

Illustrations by Beth Adams

William Morrow and Company, Inc.
New York

It is the policy of William Morrow and Company, Inc., and its imprints and affiliates, recognizing the importance of preserving what has been written, to print the books we publish on acid-free paper, and we exert our best efforts to that end.

Library of Congress Cataloging-in-Publication Data

Yalof, Suzanne.
Getting over John Doe : a story of love, heartache, and surviving with style / Suzanne Yalof.
p.   cm.
ISBN 0-688-16201-0
1. Man-woman relationships. 2. Separation (Psychology) 3. Single women — Psychology. 4. Man-woman relationships — Humor.
5. Separation (Psychology) — Humor. I. Title.
HQ801.Y29   1999
306.7 — dc21   98-24553
CIP

Printed in the United States of America
First Edition
2   3   4   5   6   7   8   9   10

Book design by Deborah Kerner

www.williammorrow.com

To Mike

Thanks

for the

inspiration

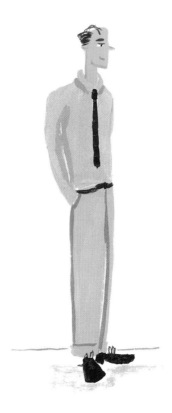

I call him

John Doe because

even though he said

he was different,

he was just like

all the rest.

Acknowledgments

I want to thank Ina Yalof and Rob Fried, who worked almost as hard on this as I did. Not only are they wonderful friends but fabulous editors. Catherine Romano was the first person I showed this to, and I thank her for telling me that it needed a point. Laura Mathews gave priceless advice and guided me to the Sandra Dijkstra Agency and to my genius agent, Steven Malk. Steven is the hippest, smartest, and most persevering agent of all time. He makes every author feel like the only one.

To Leslie and Doug Garfield, Herb, Steve and Liora Yalof, Allison Bradley Agee, Kimberely Kaye Fried, Victoria Bonomo, Paul and Deb Kogan, Inge Fonteyne, and Stephanie Hamada, thanks for not only listening to this story over and over again but for all your positive imput. Thanks to Paul Frank for his explicit explanation of the Fade Away and the Formal, and to Donald Robertson for his initial illustrations. Thanks to Beth Adams for her unbelievable art — I'm so lucky I found her. To Doris Cooper, my talented editor at William Morrow, thank you for perfecting *John Doe*. And thanks to Betty Kelly for all her support.

I

Rose-Colored

Glasses

The Pitch

It all started with my friend Sydney's description. His name was John Doe and he was open-minded, smart, funny, and once you got to know him you really didn't notice the receding hairline or even how short he was. Sydney thought we would really like each other. My gut said no.

If only I had trusted my gut.

Sydney wanted me to go to a party that Friday night at his apartment. She had been trying to get us together for months — John was one of her good friends. I kept delaying our encounter for two reasons. First, he was short and balding. And second, I was dating someone else (Evan). When I stopped dating Evan, I ran out of excuses. A party was safe enough and maybe John had cute friends. Four of my friends would be there, so it was a no-lose situation.

I figured a cameo appearance — half hour maximum — and out the door.

First Encounter

When I walked into his loft I was blown away. It was straight out of the pages of *Architectural Digest* — high ceilings, exposed pipes, white walls. A jungle of plants in every corner. It was Zen. Sparse, and everything had its place. My first thought was *"Homosexual."*

John was greeting guests as I eyed him across the room. After Sydney's description, I expected a troll. But I actually thought he was kind of attractive, in a balding sort of way, and his cool apartment made him seem a little taller.

For the most part it was a conservatively dressed crowd — men in suits, women in pearls. I was staring at a watercolor, a landscape, when I felt John come up behind me. I turned, looked into his eyes, and thought, *"Definitely not homosexual."*

We started talking as he walked me through his artwork — a Picasso (which I later learned was a print), a Miró (same story), and two Biedermeier chairs (which his ex-girlfriend took back midway through our relationship). That he would ignore his guests to spend so much time with me made me feel special.

The party started to wind down around 1:00 A.M. and only his good friend Jason and my good friend Christie remained behind. Jason and Christie were madly in love, even if it was only their second week together.

I sat on John's white canvas couch and he offered me a foot rub. My feet were killing me from my high heels, and I thought, "Why not?" Red wine, a cute boy, a foot rub in the hippest loft in SoHo — let's just say things were good.

Around 2:00 A.M. Jason and Christie wanted to go to a club. John said he would clean up his apartment and meet them there in a bit (sure), so I offered to help (sure).

We had our first kiss right there in his kitchen, surrounded by empty beer bottles.

When we finished cleaning up we were both too exhausted
to go out. He invited me to sleep over, but I declined.
That was until he offered me a pair of Brooks Brothers
men's pajamas and promised to behave. I'm a sucker for
Brooks Brothers.

Obsession

The next few weeks were a blur of bliss. I couldn't remember what life was like before John Doe. Our feelings for each other bordered on obsession. I wanted to be with him every minute he wanted to be with me. We spoke on the phone four times a day, sent e-mails to each other all day long, and had sleepovers every night. I wasn't ready to have sex and he was really sweet about it — which became an even bigger turn-on.

We would sit up all night and talk about our families. His parents insisted on good grades — mine settled for a clean room. He won Most Likely to Succeed in his high school yearbook — I was Class Clown. What did we have in common? Would you believe sushi?

I would spend all day at work fantasizing about him and would cancel all plans without hesitation.

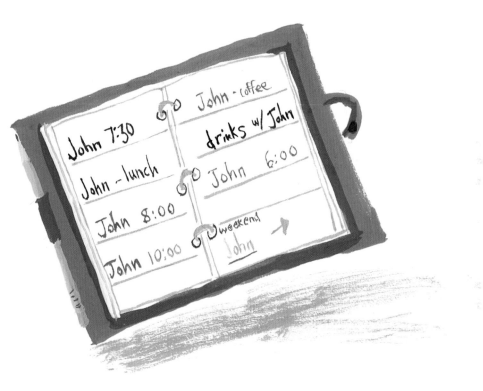

Sex

You can imagine how high my expectations were. I had thought about this moment every day for weeks. After all, he was such a great kisser and knew how to say all the right things. In my eyes he was perfect. Sex would really be the icing on the cake.

How can I say this gracefully? Okay, in my mind there are four types of sex:

Louisiana — Erotic and spicy

New York — Eclectic and sophisticated

Los Angeles — Superficial but fun

Connecticut — Predictable and bland

John was Connecticut.

A Much-Needed Break

For the first month and a half, we were together every minute that we weren't working. Each day was better than the last. So what if sex was a little predictable — I was crazy about him.

I would walk into my office every morning to find the sweetest note from him on my e-mail: *I miss u, love J* or *I can't wait to see you tonight, love J* or *I'm so happy, love J*. I would reply and he would answer me and so it went. It was wonderful.

A few friends told me I should slow down. But I blew off their suggestion. I truly believed that my situation was unique and that I knew best. (WRONG.)

I'm a fashion editor — one of the lucky few who get to go to Milan and Paris for the collections twice a year. It's truly a dream job, definitely worth the four years of hard labor that it took me to get here.

It was time for my three-week trip to Europe, and although I hated to leave John I knew it would be good to take a breather.

I arrived at my hotel across the Atlantic and found the sweetest fax from John waiting for me. For the rest of my trip I awoke to a John fax every morning. No one had ever paid so much attention to me in my entire life.

In Europe the dinners were phenomenal, the fashion shows inspiring, and my hotel — fresh flowers, the most fragrant soaps, and a view of the Eiffel Tower.

I couldn't wait to go home.

The L Word

When I returned from Europe things were even better.
We would dine at the most romantic restaurants, like La
Jumelle, La Grenouille, and La Goulue. Or we would just
hang out at one of our apartments, make pasta puttanesca,
and rent *Manhattan*. We talked about how lucky we both
felt to have met each other; we talked about timing and
how important it is in a relationship. We talked about a lot
of things that in my mind alluded to a future we would
someday share together.

I would be lying if I said that I didn't say it (the *L* word)
first. We were curled up on my sofa watching *Total Recall*
when I took the plunge. I couldn't help it. It was on the
tip of my tongue and it had to come out.

I was so relieved when he repeated the three magic words
back to me.

We used the *L* word every day after that.

That little word had big implications.

The Parents

I had a six-month rule: no introductions to parents before six months. Why should they get excited if it wasn't a sure thing? It was bad enough that my mother went into wedding-planning mode just from hearing about him in our weekly conversations. But the main reason for my not wanting to introduce him or any boyfriend to my mother is this: When she doesn't like someone, it influences my judgment. In other words, one of her looks and I'm over him. This was going so well, I didn't want to risk it.

My rule became a joke between John and me. Most men would be happy not to have to deal with their girlfriend's parents, but not John. The six-month rule only made him want to meet them more. He would ask daily — half joking, half serious. One time I let him speak to her on the phone and he said, "Ina (aka Mom), Suzy is trying to keep us apart. Want to set up a secret rendezvous?" Needless to say, she loved it until I told her that if she even entertained the idea I would put myself up for adoption.

I relented after four months. When my parents came to town we all had dinner.

There was a serious thirty-minute question-and-answer period. What did he do? (She knew but she wanted to hear it from him.) Did he have a future there? Did he want to stay on the East Coast? What did his parents do? Etc.

As I watched him answer every question with ease, I felt the smile on my face grow wider. My mother liked him — I could see it in her eyes. He aced the mom test.

Mergers and Acquisitions

By month six the *L* word was as familiar as "Good morning." The truth? I began thinking more and more about the *M* word. He certainly gave me all the signs that he was thinking about it too. For example:

- John had dreams of owning a town house. So on Sundays he would circle pictures from the paper and ask me if I would live there.

- He asked me to move in with him. I declined.

- He bought me three bars of Dove (our taste in soaps didn't jibe), a tube of Crest, and a blow-dryer to

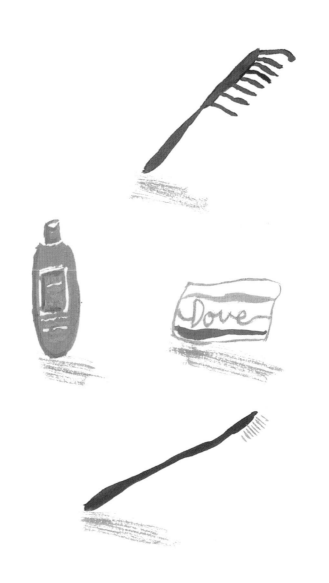

keep in his apartment. He urged me to keep my moisturizer, makeup, and a pair of jeans there. It was clear he wanted to facilitate my staying.

- He told me how much his friends loved spending time with me. They thought I was funny, fun, and daring. He said his parents and sister thought I was sweet, and good for him. He himself said that everyone told him he should marry me.

Was I so wrong to jump to conclusions?

Out to Sea

John and two couples he knew from college wanted to
take a sailing trip through the British Virgin Islands. John
loved sailing and he told me that he wanted me to love it
too because he planned on owning a boat in the future. I
didn't tell him that several years back I went on a deep-sea
fishing excursion and was so sick that the boat had to turn
around.

I was nauseated already: four strangers, eight days
trapped on a boat. I tried to get out of it by saying I
couldn't afford the trip. But then John offered to pay for
everything. It would be my thirtieth-birthday present.
I bit my tongue and accepted his invitation with faked
enthusiasm.

I have to admit the boat was impressive. It was a
hundred-foot white yacht with bright blue sails and
a teak deck, sitting there at the dock surrounded by the
bluest water I have ever seen. I was really excited about
the next eight days.

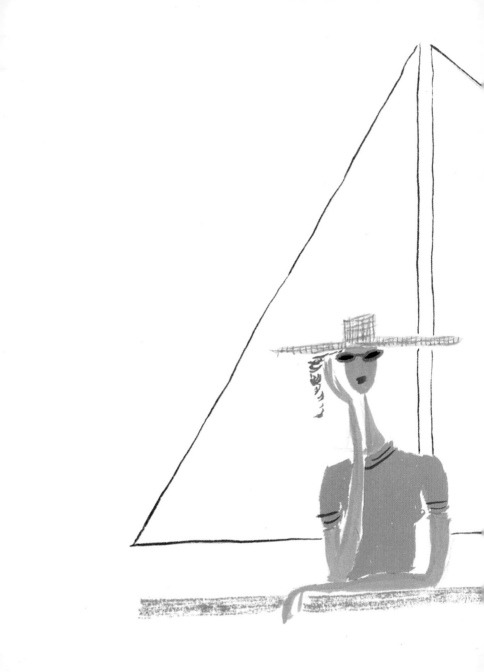

Within the first hour I found out that I wasn't the first girl to go on this trip with John. It must have slipped when Lara, one of the wives, said that she liked me much more than the last one.

By the end of the second day we had drifted into uncharted waters. He was no longer my sweet John, but Captain John Doe, sir.

He started complaining: My showers were too long (at 120 seconds — I clocked it). I used too much water when I washed the dishes (no problem — I let him do them). I didn't pack the refrigerator properly (did he want it alphabetized?). I wasn't interested enough in the "jib halyard."

I wanted off — badly! He made me uncomfortable. I had hours upon hours to stew. He must have noticed by the third day because he did a Jekyll and Hyde. Coffee was delivered to me in the morning. We stopped on islands so I could take a long hot shower. He asked me what I wanted for dinner. John calmed down and became so sweet that I felt like I was on the Love Boat. We bonded again and I felt like we had weathered the storm. I was happy I went on the trip.

Little did I know that it was the beginning of the end.

II

The

Breakup

The Clues

It was so subtle, I hardly noticed: We started going Dutch on dinners. He handed me my Valentine's Day flower (notice the singular) in person, and it looked like it had been plucked from his secretary's desk. The phone calls went from six a day to one. He was acting a little distant and started going to the gym.

There are two types of breakups. The FADE AWAY and the FORMAL.

The FADE AWAY is when the phone calls go from six a day to every other day to none. The dinners and sleepovers get spread apart until all of a sudden you realize you are not dating anymore.

The FORMAL is when you have the guts to be confrontational.

John was using the FADE AWAY. I didn't catch on immediately.

The Formal

It was February 16, and I was still kind of hurt about the
flower thing. John is a Wall Street trader — he could
afford to buy some flowers. His excuse was that he didn't
have the time, but think about it: New York City on
Valentine's Day — they sell flowers on every corner.
Something was up.

On the eve of Valentine's Day John and I drove up to his
ski house in Stowe, Vermont, for a romantic weekend. I
never expected the FORMAL riding on a chairlift, forty
feet above the snow on a mountain in Stowe. He turned to
me and said, "Suzy, I don't think I want to have children."
(Interesting . . . we had discussed wanting to name our
firstborn Max three weeks prior.) Suddenly I realized
what he was trying to do, so I looked at him through my
foggy rose-colored goggles and said, "What are you trying
to say here?"

For six months we had been together every day without so
much as a single argument. Then, out of the blue, on a
chairlift he said to me that a "little voice" in his head told

him that it just wasn't right. He couldn't say why. There was no logical reason. It was just that "little voice," and he had to be true to it.

It was obvious he wanted to end it, but did he have to make that "little voice" the fall guy? I sat in the cold sky in shock, looking down at the skiers below. I mean, I thought he was the one and now I had to accept that he wasn't. Even worse, I had to face the reality that *he* dumped *me*.

For six months that same "little voice" had told him to e-mail me every hour on the hour to say he loved me. It said that I was the perfect woman for him and that it thought I was the "one." Now I wanted to smack that "little voice."

A Long Ride Home

When we returned to the ski house I packed my bag and told him to take me home. There is nothing like being dumped and having a five-hour drive home together ahead of you.

I had five hours to dwell. I couldn't stop obsessing over him or over the fact that I had really thought this was it and it wasn't. It didn't help that I had just turned thirty, and all the women I had thought no one would ever marry were dropping like flies.

What was wrong with me? I analyzed myself: Should I have played harder to get? Should I have pretended to be someone else? Was I too nice? Was I too social? Was I too independent? Was I not domestic enough? Was I too driven? Was it my lifestyle? Was I too outgoing?

There was no answer. All I knew was that I was played and he was the player and that this was the longest drive of my life.

Divesting and Repossessing

When we arrived home John helped me bring my bags up
to my apartment. Then I excused myself, left him standing
in the foyer, and gathered every article of his clothing. I
shoved his underwear, shoes, shirts, and newly pressed
suit into a ball, placed it in a bag, and dropped it at his
feet. He stood there, in the middle of the foyer, looking
down at his belongings. Then he looked up and said,
"You forgot my cuff links."

It was really over.

The Second Coming

Well, not quite. A week later I got a three-page letter from John pleading with me to try again. He said he had made a mistake and had been too quick to end it. I told him he could come over but asked him to bring my boots, my dress, my toiletries, my two sweaters, and anything else I had left at his house. When he arrived we talked: He missed me, loved me, and didn't know that little voice anymore. We cried: He was confused, scared, and had almost lost the one thing he really cared about. We went for a long walk through Central Park, held hands, and wallowed in couplehood all over again. I agreed to try once more.

So there I was, my fantasy realized — he came crawling back and we were fooling around like nothing had ever happened. Then I noticed a strange look on his face, so I asked him, "What's up?" To which he replied, "Suzy, I should be the happiest person in the world, but I'm not. It's that 'little voice' saying don't do this. Can't explain it."

That little shit broke up with me twice.

Have the Last Word

After the breakup John wrote me a couple of letters to say
how sorry he was and why he had to trust his "little voice."
He reiterated our differences: *I* didn't like sailing enough
. . . *I* wasn't as neat as he was . . . *I* wanted sex more than
twice a week, etc. Then he had the nerve to ask for my
friendship. I guess breaking up twice wasn't enough
for him.

After his third letter it was time for *me* to have the last
word. So I wrote him a note. The idea was to hide my real
feelings (completely devastated and depressed), be cold,
and tell him to screw off without actually saying it:

> *Dear John,*
> *I don't see why you feel the continual need to tell me*
> *I'm not right for you. I got it the first five times. Give*
> *up the idea of being friends. It won't happen. You see,*
> *while you were having your "inner conflict," I was*
> *walking around happy — in love. When I found out*
> *that we were having two different relationships, it blew*
> *my mind. Let's move on.*
>
> *Suzy*

Sending it off felt good . . . but not good enough. So I
wrote him the meanest letters ever written and sent those
to myself. It felt great to open them up and read them. I
fantasized about what his reaction would have been. I was
so happy I never sent those letters to him. He never would
have appreciated them as much as I did.

Tear Up Everything That Reminds You of Him

When I called my best friend, Allison, and read her the latest John letter she said to give her five minutes. She canceled her plans and came running over immediately. I guess she could tell how upset I was — this was her fourth visit that week. She reread all of his letters and told me what an idiot he was (like any good friend would). She said, "Suzy, you're *too* dynamic, *too* independent, *too* smart — men want women who make *them* feel good." According to her I was overqualified.

Allison went into my closet and pulled out two black dresses, a short satin slip dress and a long velvet halter dress, and told me to put on one. I chose the slip, she put on the halter. Then Allison and I, all in black, went into my bathroom with candles and incense. We prepared for a ceremony: dimmed the lights, removed the towels and toiletries. I tore his letter into tiny little pieces and we screamed, "Take that, John Doe," as the shredded paper slowly twisted down the toilet. We proceeded to tear up every photo of him and every letter he'd written.

I was worried my toilet would overflow.

The Housekeeper

I woke one morning and, as I had every morning for the
past month, wondered: Is John Doe waking up thinking
of me? My housekeeper, who cleans his house too, told me
that he wasn't as compulsively neat as usual. Did that
mean he was depressed? I was reaching for information
anywhere I could get it. I even thought about giving her
a raise and having her do some real work for me. My
imagination went wild. But then she mentioned something
about ethics and client confidentiality and I knew to back
off. (Funny . . . I didn't know she went to law school in
between vacuuming and dusting.)

III

Things
I Wish
I Had Known
Then

Don't Go Changing to Try to Please Him

The more time I spent with John, the more I wanted to be like him. I even redecorated my apartment so it would please him aesthetically. I thought it was for me at the time, but after the breakup I saw what a mistake I'd made. My apartment was so colorful before, yellow walls, navy-striped curtains, and coral sofas. Now it was all shades of beige. I was living in a cream puff.

Occasionally I would cook for John — I pretended to know what I was doing and that I loved cooking. That was until I got caught by his friend Nick putting pasta into water that hadn't reached the boiling point. Nick just looked at me and said, "I'm wise to your lies."

Never Trust a Man Who Talks About Marriage in the First Three Months

After three months with John I thought my search was over. He was everything I was looking for: sweet, smart, funny, cute but not too cute, successful, open-minded, and adventurous. We loved the same food, Thai and Japanese; listened to the same music, from R & B to alternative to James Taylor. And we were both open-minded to spirituality, from flotation tanks to transcendental meditation. He even had the same book I had, *Out of the Body in 30 Days: A Guide to Astral Projection*. Really — what are the chances of that?

The e-mails, the faxes, the love letters, the *L* word, the parents, our friends, and the constant talk about the uniqueness of our relationship all contributed to my fantasies about the *M* word.

The point is this: *He* built up my expectations and then *he* got scared when I had them. There is something to be said for those affectionate but silent types.

Hold Out on Re-Wardrobing Him
Until There Is a Ring
on Your Finger

When I met John he needed serious help in the wardrobe
department. After the third month, I took him to J.P. Tod's
and got him a decent pair of shoes. I also went with him to
Barneys and helped him pick out shirts and explained how
to wear them. When I was through with him he looked
like a new man. There were no more patterned sweaters,
and the sweatpants had made it into the garbage can. I
filled him with confidence, telling him he looked great all
the time. He walked tall, looked good, and believed his
own press. I did all the dirty work and now some other
woman would reap the benefits.

Don't Be So Available

Why should I play by the rules? I felt secure in our relationship, so I used to stay with John at least five nights a week. We would play odds or evens and shoot for which apartment to stay at. We lived on opposite ends of the city, but we wanted to be together and made concessions. I ended up staying in his apartment 90 percent of the time.

Before we started dating I was out every night of the week. When I met John I put my life on hold. I wanted to be available for him whenever he wanted me. Did I make his life too easy? Did he get bored?

You are probably sitting there doubting yourself, thinking it was you. But how about this theory: There are just a lot of frogs out there. So even if you are dying to be with him every night, even if you really think you are different from all the rest of us — don't do it.

IV

What I Did
That Made
Me Feel
Better

Do All the Things He Always Hated

- Stop and ask several strangers for directions.
- Change your order at least four times before deciding on what to eat.
- Don't shave your legs for a week.
- Wear a low-cut blouse and a tight pencil skirt and go to a place where you know you will see his friends — and flirt.
- Stay on the phone with a girlfriend for an hour.
- Eat beef jerky.
- Listen to show tunes and sing along at the top of your lungs.

But most important: Stop questioning yourself. You must never lose perspective — it's all *his* fault.

Rent a Video and Have a Good Cry

It was the first Friday after the breakup and I was home alone in my pajamas at 7 P.M., eating Chinese food out of the carton. I'd rented *An Unmarried Woman*. I had always enjoyed this film and now was identifying with it like never before. *There is nothing like a good video to put life into perspective.* As I watched it I realized that if a woman as smart and beautiful as Jill Clayburgh was getting dumped, there was a problem with the way of the world, not with me.

The breakup scene in that movie is so real: Jill Clayburgh is walking down the street with her husband, glowing as she speaks of their plans for the summer. Then the camera pans in on her husband's face as he breaks into tears. He tells her he has been having an affair for the past year with a twenty-six-year-old woman he picked up in the men's shirt department at Bloomingdale's. Jill Clayburgh's expression is genius. She looks shocked, furious, nauseated, and repulsed all at the same time. The next scene finds her at a bar with her friends drowning her sorrows. As she's leaving the bar, a man smiles at her and says, "Hello." She looks at him and replies, "Fuck you."

I love that scene!

Edit Your Words

When John and I broke up, it was all I talked about.
I would step into an
elevator and someone
would press 2 and I
would say to this
complete stranger,
"You know, that
reminds me of my
ex-boyfriend. He
lived on the second
floor." I was so
boring. I couldn't
stand listening to myself. My friends
were sweet to put up with me. Finally, when I just couldn't
impose on them anymore, I decided to take my anger out
on paper instead of exhausting my friends and strangers.
He was stuck in my mind, and writing about him was the
only thing I could do to get him out and restore my sanity.

The thought of writing a book and talking to Oprah about
it was much more interesting than dating John ever was.
Find your medium!

Contact All the Men Who
Still Love You

I needed an ego boost, so the first thing I did was call
several of my ex-boyfriends. I even went out for dinner
with two of them.

I must admit, I had a great evening with both guys. I
flirted shamelessly. Although I had no desire to rekindle
the romance, it felt great to know that I was still desirable.

Most people will tell you that seeing old boyfriends is a
mistake, but it always makes me feel a lot better. Being
liked when you don't like back can be empowering.
Sometimes it is best to contact men who live far away, so
you never have to worry about actually dealing with them
face-to-face.

Get Rid of the Gift

John gave me a silver and gold twisted bangle for
Christmas. I was incredibly touched that he would go out
of his way to find something so special. When he slipped it
on my hand he said, "I love you so much, pumpkin." I used
to gaze for hours at my wrist and smile.

After the split I hated that bracelet. I dwelled on what to
do with it. I even thought of sending it back to him, but I
thought that might make him happy, so I didn't.

Then, one morning when I was waiting for the subway, I
saw a homeless woman. She was wearing a tattered man's
overcoat and a gray wool skirt over torn pants. I told her
that it would mean so much to me if she would wear the
bracelet and not sell it for at least a week. She agreed and
quickly put it on.

I looked at the bracelet on *her* wrist and it made me smile.

Get Back at Him by Taking It
Out on a Stranger Who Deserves It

Any man in my path became a ticket to getting back at John Doe. One of my friends, Joe, tried to set me up with his friend Alberto. My friend Stephanie warned me that he was a womanizer. I went for a drink with Joe, and Alberto was supposed to meet us. He never showed.

A few days later, at a party in Joe's apartment on the Upper West Side, Stephanie pointed out Alberto to me. He was on the terrace and I could see him through the glass. He was with a blond model. His hands were caressing her shoulders as he eyed every woman who passed. I hated him on sight. I then found myself winking and blowing him kisses through the window. He kept turning his head, trying to place me. When he came inside I approached him.

"Alberto! It's been too long," I said.

"I know. You look great. What has it been — two years?" he said.

The bastard was trying to play it off, but I could see his panic. He was searching for recall where there was none.

"Maybe two and a half. You look good too — is your hair shorter?" I said.

Then he said, "A little. So who do you know here?"

"Joe — you must remember that," I said. "Remember that time, well, you know . . . I was pretty upset you never called after."

It was clear that Alberto was flirting with me.

The blond model, without hesitation, gave him a dirty look and walked away.

Then I walked away and left him standing alone.

Later in the evening I confessed. His faced turned red and he started calling me Italian names that weren't nice, but afterward, when he calmed down, we had a good laugh. Then he was in love. I couldn't get him away from me.

I behaved cruelly and he liked me for it.

Heed Advice from the Little People

My brother called me this morning to see if I could
baby-sit Saturday night. I was over being Aunt Suzy. I
have five nieces and nephews, and both my sister and
brother feel I don't spend enough time with their kids. I
truly adore all of them. It's fun to have them over, watch
The Flintstones, and eat chocolate cake for breakfast. It's
great to be the one who always makes them smile. I don't
take away TV or put the wrong cheese on their bologna
sandwiches. I am never the villain, and they love me for it.
But the thought of being single and spending my Saturday
night with them was too much to bear. So I lied, said I was
busy, and went to the movies alone.

My sister's nine-year-old daughter, Noonie, is a real
character. I could laugh at her all day. When John and I
broke up, Noonie told me that I should close my eyes and
picture him at her age — a total nerd. She also said that
she was happy it ended. She said it was important that she
like my future husband, because it affected her life — and
she didn't like John Doe.

Shop

I bought three pairs of Manolo Blahnik shoes on sale for
$350 (they usually go for $500 a pair) and I felt good.
Shopping was great therapy and I had something to
show for it in the end. My fear was that I was becoming
addicted — a bona fide shopaholic. I was high for an hour

after each purchase. I couldn't get enough. I was depressed, but I never looked better.

A new life deserves a new wardrobe.

Live Out Your Dreams
in Your Fantasy World

I noticed that my fantasy world had changed. Before I met
John, I fantasized about winning the lottery — the big one
— and putting my parents and aunts and uncles into
retirement. I would buy an apartment overlooking Central
Park. My days were full of notions. Then I met John and
dreamed about his proposal, getting married, having
children, and retiring to a Caribbean island.

Now my fantasies were about publicly humiliating him. I
wanted to make him jealous. I imagined that he would ask
me to come back and then I would say no. I had fantasies
of being with some divine specimen and bumping into
John while he was in the midst of a horrific blind date
with an ugly duck. Then I would pretend I couldn't
remember his name, and only vaguely the face.

This was my favorite fantasy: I would be sitting in a
restaurant with Sandra Bullock, Johnny Depp, and Rick
Moranis. We would be discussing the screen adaptation of
Getting Over John Doe. Then John would come over to the

table and I would introduce him and explain that Rick was playing him in the movie.

I found myself reading his horoscope all the time (he's a Taurus). I actually got angry when his horoscope indicated a new love or any type of happiness. I was pleased when financial problems and romantic upsets appeared in his future.

Misbehave a Little

I was over my "nice girl" image. Have
you ever noticed that the most difficult
women get the sweetest husbands? It was
time to misbehave a little. So I had that
extra glass of Chardonnay and went out
dirty-dancing. Drove from New York
City to the Hamptons on the back of a
Harley-Davidson, and bought a pair of
leather jeans — it felt good to be bad.

Listen to Stories of Other Imperfect Relationships – They Will Make You Feel Much Better

I would rather be happy and single than the opposite. I had lunch with a girlfriend who is completely bored in her marriage. She had been offered a fantastic job in Los Angeles and wanted to take it, but her husband wanted to stay in cold, dirty New York City. She was tired of doing his laundry, making his meals, and listening to him tell the same stories over and over again. She hated that he needed her daily itinerary every night after dinner. She was bored with his constant affection and tired of him. She had married for practical reasons and because of his relentless pursuit. He trapped her with great gifts, decent sex, and the promise of a financially secure future. Basically, she settled. But the number one reason for marrying him was her hatred of his mother.

His mother hated her. Before they got married she went on a shopping trip with his mother and over lunch was offered enough money to travel around the world for a year and to set up an apartment when she returned. In exchange, all she had to do was leave her son alone. My friend was so angry that she married him just to get back at his mother. Now she wants a divorce but swears that she won't give his mother the satisfaction. I never appreciated being single more. I felt free.

V

Post-Breakup

Dos and

Don'ts

Don't Drink and Dial

If there is one thing that I want to stress, it is this: There is
no bigger turnoff than a woman who is slurring over the
phone begging for sex or, even worse, a reconciliation.
Unfortunately, it is something that most of us have done at
some point in our lives. I am proud to say that I didn't do
it with John Doe.

Well, not exactly, anyway. I struggled with an
overwhelming desire to make phony phone calls to him
daily. Can you imagine being thirty and still wanting to
make phony phone calls? Anyway, I was out for drinks
with my girlfriend Sam and we came up with a plan. She
was going to call John and say, "Hello, this is Sam, I'm a
good friend of Jack's [John's best friend, who had put him
up in Boston for three months years ago] and, well . . .
I'm coming to New York for a couple of months and Jack
said he was sure you would put me up for my first couple
of weeks. Is that okay?" I was so happy when his machine
picked up. She hung up the phone — no message — but
we must have laughed uncontrollably for at least an hour
thinking about what his reaction would have been. Can
you imagine how embarrassed I would have been if he had
answered the phone and known I was behind it? Alcohol
and telephones don't mix.

Never Let On to His Friends That You Care

I was so happy to finally bump into Larissa, one of John's friends. Larissa was the wife of Kevin, John's college roommate. We used to double-date. There was no question about it — she was *his* friend.

It was midafternoon on a Sunday somewhere in the Eighties on Madison Avenue. She was walking alone, shopping bags in hand, when I spotted her. Before hellos were even exchanged I had an overwhelming desire to pump Larissa for information. Fortunately, Allison was there and gave me one of her "don't even go there" looks. So I put on my best face and showed no signs of the devastation I occasionally still felt. We exchanged how-are-you's, talked a little about the weather and our mutual friend Lida. Larissa ended our three-minute superficial conversation with the inappropriately appropriate "Let's get together." Allison said that I was perfectly indifferent.

I spent the rest of the week wondering if she would or wouldn't tell him we saw each other. Would she say I looked good? That I seemed happy? I was proud I hadn't let on that I cared.

Take Advantage of All Opportunities That Will Preoccupy You

It was the weekend that John and I were supposed to attend his friend's wedding in Mississippi. John would be there and so would my two friends Sydney and Christie. I was praying that Sydney wouldn't let on that I had told her every detail of the breakup, but at the same time I wanted her to get as much information from him as possible.

When I was invited to go to Vermont that same weekend, I jumped at the opportunity. A house full of good friends, robust wine, and a roaring fireplace that overlooked a snow-covered mountain sounded like heaven. Anything to get my mind off him and *that* wedding. Snowmobiling at 50 mph was just what the doctor ordered. I drove back to New York feeling relaxed and happy.

Use Mutual Friends as Spies and Make Sure Their Report Back Is Negative

I couldn't wait. I had to call Sydney immediately to find out all the details of the wedding weekend. I don't know what I expected to hear. I *wanted* to hear that he had had some regrets and was a little depressed. Certainly not the news that she told me. Apparently, the whole weekend, John was slobbering all over someone he had just met — a loose bimbo. As if this wasn't bad enough, he committed P.D.A. on the dance floor in front of the bride's parents in their home. He'd had a couple too many cocktails and apparently was a sight to behold. On top of this, he dressed inappropriately for the brunch the following day — jeans and a sweater when all the other men were in sport jackets and ties. I have heard stories of women being completely snowed over, but I never expected to be one of them. How could the man I thought was so wonderful be so tacky?

Celebrate His Romantic Upsets

I had dinner with another spy and was quite satisfied with her information. She told me that after returning to New York, John went on a date with the same girl he was all over at the wedding, and she rejected him. *Joy* was not strong enough to describe my feelings. *Elation* was closer to it.

I also felt a certain envy because she had figured out in one date what it took me six months to understand. I upgraded her from a loose bimbo to a liberated woman with street smarts.

Use Mutual Friends as Messengers and Make Sure Their Report to Your Ex Is Positive

It is imperative that your friends memorize their scripts before bumping into your ex. The script I prepared for my friends went something like this: "Suzy? Oh, she just bought the sweetest town house downtown [*he's always wanted one*]. None of us could believe it when her Web site took off [*he's been working on a Web site unsuccessfully for a year*], it was like magic. She has been seeing this investment banker [*John is a trader*] who actually works in your firm. I don't remember his name, but he kind of looks like Antonio Sabato. You know, from the Calvin ads. I think they are sailing around the Galápagos Islands this week [*he always wanted to do that trip*]. Anyway — how are you? Ooh, look at the time. Nice seeing you. Gotta run. Bye."

Stay Away from Oreos

After the breakup I had an insatiable appetite. I could not get enough of all the foods I had last eaten when I was in seventh grade — Yodels, Twinkies, those pink fluffy things, Mallomars, and Ring-Dings. It was the worst. Not only was I depressed but I felt fat. The only thing that stopped me was the thought of bumping into him.

Don't Ask Questions You Don't Want the Answer To

I came in to work one morning to learn that Sarah, one of the women in my office, had seen John the night before at a party. The mere mention of his name made me crumble. She told me that they spoke. He said "Hi" and she said "Hi" back.

Well, that was it. It didn't matter what he said. It was enough of an excuse, in my mind, to justify calling him. It was Good Friday and he was home. I told him that I didn't want to be angry at him anymore. Then I foolishly asked questions.

> *Me:* "What was the real reason?"
>
> *Him:* "I knew that I didn't want to spend the rest of my life with you, but I felt bad because you were so in love with me." Ouch.
>
> *Me:* "Are you dating?" (Stupid question.)
>
> *Him:* "Uh, yes, two people. Remember that girl I was dating before you? Well . . . she's really nice." Ouch.
>
> *Me:* "Have you been upset at all?"

Him: "Well, I guess the first two weeks were
difficult. But then I went to Aspen, had fun,
and felt much better. Have you ever been
to Aspen?"

His words came at me like darts. I probably should have
just said good-bye, but I couldn't. Instead, I reminded him
that he was the one who asked *me* to move in, he was the
one who told *me* I was perfect for him, and *he* was the one
who e-mailed *me* love letters every day. I told him I was
writing a book about him and asked if I could use his
name. His response was "Sure, you can use it. No one
would ever think it was me." He was so egotistical, he
probably took it as a compliment.

When he asked me if he could set me up with anyone,
I knew it was time to hang up.

Keep Only One Photo of Him, the Ugliest One Ever Taken

On the wall in my office I hung the ugliest photo of John I could find. On top of it I drew a mustache, goatee, thick eyebrows, and devil ears. But I could still see his eyes. I couldn't help but think, "How could he not be in love with me?"

Limit Conversations with Mom

My mother became my therapist. But at the same time her advice was annoying. She was, after all, my mother. I told her stories about boring, inarticulate men to whom I had no sexual attraction and she told me that I was too picky.

Before I turned thirty, no one was good enough. Now if he had two legs and was heterosexual, he was a catch. I felt like Rhoda Morgenstern. I knew Mom felt bad for me, but her hiding it made me feel worse. She is the best mother in the world, but a realist to a fault. Sometimes you need to hear lies. She would say, "Suzy, maybe he just knew that he didn't want to marry you." Whose side was she on, anyway? I preferred my version — that he was a total moron.

Sometimes I can see my own thoughts by looking in her eyes. I was pathetic and dwelling, and we both knew it. I was really looking forward to the moment when we could look back and laugh about it.

Beware of Pickup Locations

I hate obvious pickup places — you know, those certain
bars, clubs, restaurants, beaches, share houses, and
religious mixers where you feel like a piece of sirloin.
The intentions are so transparent. Women looking for
husbands. Men looking for sex. A lot of money being spent
with very low return. The lines are so thick and obvious,
I feel like every man thinks I'm an idiot for even listening
to him.

I always find that an atmosphere conducive to meeting
eligible men is the worst place to meet them. I am usually
luckier finding love in the local video store.

VIDEOS

Get Rid of Your Worst Qualities

When I was really down I called my good friend Dirk to ask him what he thought men truly wanted. "To find a lady," he said. Dirk was my water-ski partner with whom I occasionally did shots, smoked cigars, and shared all my dirtiest jokes. I looked around at all my taken girlfriends, and it was true! They were into nails, hair, makeup, facials, home improvement, and "girlie-girl" things.

I decided to change. Okay, I'd give up cigars, toss my old running shoes, get a manicure, and fix up my apartment. If finding Mr. Right meant the application of eye shadow, then so be it.

I thought about all the things I did that irritated John — the occasional cigarette I smoked, my love of McDonald's, and my avoidance of the gym. So I quit smoking, started ordering in from Great American Health Bar, and went to the gym religiously to get back at him. Perhaps this breakup was the best thing ever to happen to me.

Be Prepared for When He Calls – They Always Do

Carry a three-by-five index card with you at all times, itemizing everything you want to say, just in case.

When John called, it couldn't have been better timing. My mother was staying with me, so even if I wanted to, I couldn't start too heavy a conversation because she would give me such grief afterward, it wouldn't be worth it. She answered the phone and told me it was him.

The conversation went like this:

Him: "Hi, Suzy. It's John. Was that your mother?"
Me: "Yes." (That must have freaked him out a little.)
Him: "I have two questions for you. The first is: How are you?"
Me: "Fine."
Him: "The second is: Are you really writing a book called *Getting Over* —— [his real first name], or is that just a joke?"
Me: "It's just a joke. Is that it?"

Him: "Yes."
Me: "Good-bye." I hung up.

YES! I had mastered the phone call! I hung up on him
without actually hanging up on him. I spent all night
awake, reenacting the conversation with different
punch lines.

Here is what I wish I had said:

"John who?"

"No, it wasn't my mother, it was my girlfriend —
I thought they told you."

"Yes, I am writing a book, but the title is *F*#* You,
John Doe.*"

and on

and on

and on

Stay Away from His Neighborhood

. . . unless you are totally prepared to deal with him. I felt high anxiety when I passed his apartment. It was as if I was on LSD. Every man, woman, child, and animal had his face. Bad trip!

Use Work as an Outlet:
Get Mad and Get a Promotion

When I was madly in love, my work came second. Now, without him, I was turning into a workaholic. In at 8:00 A.M., out on business dinners every night. I bonded with anyone who had an expense account. Work was an outlet and I plugged myself in. My boss was thrilled.

VI

Dating

Find Your Blind-Date Mantra

I had to prepare myself for blind dates. I had a mantra and it was the way I kept myself calm. Right before a date I would say over and over in my head, "This is a business meeting and the only good thing to come out of it will be a great meal." If I liked my date it was a nice surprise, and if

this is a business meeting
this is a business meeting
this is a business meeting
this is a business meeting
this is a business meeting
this is a business meeting
this is a business meeting
this is a business meeting
this is a business meeting
this is a business meeting

I didn't, it wasn't a letdown. I always had fun with this attitude and my dates usually liked me because they sensed that I didn't care too much about finding a husband (I guess I hid it well).

Blind-Dating

Right after the breakup the yentas went to work.
Everybody wanted to set me up. I felt like 1-800-DIAL-
A-DATE: "Hi, this is Ron Saks. I'm a friend of a friend
of a friend."

I met Ron for dinner. He was tall, dark, handsome, and a
graduate of Princeton — a doctor. Over dinner he told me
the story of his life starting from third grade. I was given a
history lesson on his love life. I felt like we were in therapy
— *I* was the doctor, *he* was the patient. I felt like *he* should
have paid *me* at the end of the evening for the advice. I felt
like *he* should have been lying on a leather couch.

Even though our date ranked as one of the top five worst
dates I'd ever had, Ron eventually set me up with one of
his very cute friends. So be nice to everyone — you never
know who their friends are.

If You're Not Interested, Give Him a Good-Night Handshake – and Other Ways of Getting Out Of It

I really wanted to like Boris Yablonsky, but I didn't. You know how you can be sitting across from someone and it's an effort just to have a conversation? I felt like I had to fill the airspace, so I shared stories I shouldn't have. My fear of flying, interoffice politics, my belief in reincarnation. A little much for a first date. Boris had great qualities, but I wasn't into him. One pet peeve of mine is poor diction. Boris didn't pronounce his *g*'s — goin', doin', seein' — he was history. Then there is the wine test. I needed a lot of it — not a good sign.

I learned something that night. Don't drink too much when you know you don't like him. The booze goggles made me a little flirtatious and he became hopeful. When he called the next morning I realized that I must have sent mixed signals and that he didn't get the "good-night handshake" at the end of the evening.

Here are three ways to guarantee that there will not be a second date:

1. Sleep with him.
2. Talk about marriage.
3. Tell him you are insanely busy for the next three weeks and can he try to call after that. Then, when he calls, tell him you're insanely busy for the next three weeks and can he call you after that.

Repeat as needed.

The Pitch Versus the Reality

When I arrived home from my evening with Boris,
the first thing I did was rush to the phone hoping there
would be a message from John. I had five messages. They
were all from Allison. She had gone from being my best
friend to being my marriage broker. She had found the
perfect man for me. The message said he was thirty-one,
Jewish, and a producer at *Dateline*. His name was David
Cohen, and she wanted a finder's fee. She was rambling:
He was an impeccable dresser, smart, superfunny, and
romantic. He was tan (did that mean he was ugly?). A
typical date consisted of dinner at Chez George (really
romantic) with fine wine. What could I say? YES!

Here is how our date went. First off, we met at a bar —
there was no food or wine in sight. In fact, if I hadn't
suggested that we eat, we would have been drinking beer
on tap all night. Second, his suit was so baggy, it was
either borrowed or he had recently dropped a hundred
pounds. Okay, he was tan, and nice enough. But that's not
nice enough.

I wish I could have honest answers to the following questions before consenting to date a stranger:

1. What was the longest relationship you ever had?
2. What was *her* side of the story? Can I have her phone number?
3. What is your relationship with your mother like?
4. Are you happy with your job? Does it affect your sex life?
5. Do you have a criminal record?
6. Do you want to get married before you die?

Trust Your Instincts

The thing I hate most about being single is that everyone gets annoyed when you meet a good man and you don't like him. Just because I'm single doesn't mean I will have a relationship with *anyone*. Would they? There has to be some physical attraction accompanying a good résumé. "Give him a chance," they say, but can I help it if he whistles his *s*'s? Who cares if he's a doctor when you can't kiss him.

Trust your instincts — if you don't like him, then you don't like him. It's your life, not theirs. Simple.

The FIDO Philosophy

The phone rang at 7:30 A.M., and I knew it was my mother. She wanted to hear all about my date the night before. When I clearly stated that I didn't like him, she asked if I would go out with him again. *Hello!*

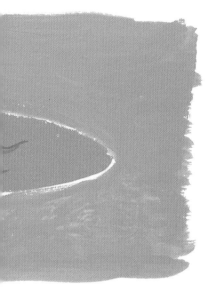

Then she got angry that I was still thinking about John. "Have you ever heard of the FIDO philosophy?" she asked (knowing full well I hadn't, because she had just heard about it herself). She explained, "When you play golf and someone's ball goes into the woods, everyone rides around in their golf cart to look for it. After about five minutes with no success, it's 'FIDO' (Fuck It, Drive On)." Mother's little wisdom always hits home.

Date a Man You Would Never Bring Home

I was tired of thinking that every guy had to be "The Guy." Dating was starting to feel like work — except I like work more.

There was only one thing left to do. Date a man I was sure my mother would hate. Being a little rebellious always cheers me up. His name was Stephano and he could barely (I'm being kind here) speak English. He was so sexy in that bad-boy kind of way. You know the type, long hair, dark skin, dark brown eyes — *hot*. But deep down inside, there were only two things he wanted from me, one of which was a green card. Still, riding on the back of his Harley was a much-needed break from the standard informational interview dates I had begun to loathe.

When dating stops being fun, take a break. There will always be men out there.

VII

The

Confrontation

The Invite

Just when I was starting to feel better I got the call. Christie and Jason, the couple who met two weeks before John and I started dating, were engaged. Steve, Jason's brother, was throwing an engagement party. He left a message on my machine saying that he, his brothers, and Christie hoped I would come even if John Doe would definitely be there. I imagined all our friends wanted to witness the reunion — the drama.

It was so Roman.

They (who, I don't know) say that it takes half the time you dated a person to get over him. The party would hit almost to the day — three months later. The timing was perfect. I would put it all to the test: see him and have a normal conversation — not care. I would have closure.

I called back and left a message: "Of course I will be there! Can't wait! And by the way, who is John Doe?"

Who: *Christie and Jason*

Why: *to celebrate their engagement*

Where: *Steve's loft*

1001 Spring Street, Apt. J

When: *Friday, July 3rd, 8.00 p.m.*

The Preparation

This will be the event you replay in your mind for the next few weeks, so don't blow it. Be prepared.

I had a week to memorize my script and drop five pounds. I rehearsed all the possible scenarios, to make sure I would emerge victorious. I thought about bringing a date but decided against it. I felt it would seem like I was trying too hard — it would look too deliberate. No, I was going solo — strong.

It took me three hours to get dressed. Everything in my closet was either on my bed, on the floor, or on me three times. I must say I looked pretty good in the end. Tight cream sleeveless top and matching cream pants. Thank God it was a good hair day! On the ride down "I Will Survive" came on the radio. I never really took in the lyrics before, but I always knew the words. I found myself singing each word with feeling until I saw the cabdriver shake his head as he looked at me in his rearview mirror.

I was so nervous, but the six-flight walk up calmed me down. I was proud that I made it in my four-inch heels.

The Engagement Party

Here is what I would like to say happened at the party:

  1. He saw me walk through the door and came
  slithering across the floor on his belly.

2. I extended my hand and helped him stand up.
3. We looked deeply into each other's eyes.
4. I said, "Later," and walked away.

Here is what really happened:

1. He came in with another woman on his arm.
2. He was wearing the shirt I'd picked out and the shoes I'd bought for him.
3. After he ignored me for the first two hours, I couldn't resist anymore. I walked over to him, not sure what for or what to expect. Suddenly I forgot all my lines and started belittling him (didn't plan on it, but couldn't help it).
4. I then turned to his date and said, "We have to talk." I watched his jaw drop to the floor and I broke into an uncontrollable fit of laughter.
5. I walked away and made myself a rum and diet Coke.

An Affair to Remember

It was the weekend of Christie and Jason's wedding, two months after the engagement party, and I was feeling really good.

I promised myself that I would not talk to John and would stay as far away as possible. This was Christie's day and I really wanted to enjoy their wedding. I must admit I was a little embarrassed about the way I acted at the engagement party and I swore (if only to myself) not to make a repeat performance.

Christie and Jason looked gorgeous and so happy together. It was great to see all of my friends and some of the friends I had made through John at the wedding. Most of John's friends came up to me at one point or another to say that they missed spending time together.

Sweet Christie sat me at the best table. Seven of the cutest single men at the wedding and only three single women (myself included). I danced every dance.

As I danced to "You Dropped the Bomb on Me," I noticed John Doe out of the corner of my eye. I had actually forgotten he was there until I saw him struggling with his rhythm. He was the worst dancer. I looked back at my adorable dance partner and then looked at John Doe.

I didn't remember him being so short.

The End

The Getting Over John Doe Sound Track

"I'm Not Bitter, I Just Wish You Were Dead"

"Looking for a New Love"

"I'm on a Plane"

"Enough Is Enough"

"I Will Survive"

"You Dropped the Bomb on Me"

"It's Too Late"

"Tainted Love"

"Freedom"

"Been Around the World"

"Never Can Say Good-bye"

"You're So Vain"